CONTENTS

Who is Spider-Man?   6

Super-powers - Super-tricky!   26

Those mean, sly bad guys!   52

I ♥ SCIENCE

PP & MJ 4EVA

FRIENDLY NEIGHBOURHOOD SPIDER-MAN

DAILY BUGLE SPIDER-MAN!

Growing up Spidey   76

WEBSLINGERS UNITE!

THWIP!

Swinging it   96

Glossary   122

Acknowledgements   128

R.I.P. UNCLE BEN

THOK!

Who is SPIDER-MAN?

SUPER

We all know what they're like, right?

"STRONG" — Powerful

SUPER CONFIDENT

You'd probably use the word **awesome!**

And most of the time you'd be right. But right here, right now, we are going to talk about a Super Hero who is a little different from your average awesome Super Hero.

HEROES

We are talking about a skinny little guy named **Peter Parker.** You may have heard of him. He is

Spider-Man!

Spider-Man is brave, sure. He has defeated loads of **scary villains.** But Peter Parker? Looking at him, you wouldn't have a clue…

MEET PETER.

Average hair

Average face

Average height

Average clothes

He's just a **regular guy,** the boy next door, an AVERAGE JOE, a — you get the picture.

He grew up in **New York city.** He goes to school, but it's not much fun for him (more on that later).

Yes, he has homework. No, he's not good at sports.

Can't you catch?!

Whoops!

Let's be honest, Peter is a bit of a

SCIENCE nerd!

$e=mc^2$

And as useful and important as science is, most of the kids at Peter's school think it's

JUST. NOT. COOL.

That's a shame for Peter, because it means that most kids think he is **JUST. NOT. COOL** either. Don't worry, Peter, we think you're cool!

Peter lives with his **Uncle Ben** and *Aunt May.*

Peter's parents died in a plane crash when he was young, so he kind of thinks of Uncle Ben and Aunt May as his **parents.** And they love him like a son.

Makes New York's best pancakes

Awesome dude

Uncle Ben used to be in the military police, so he knows all about being brave and doing the right thing.

He was also once a **singer** in a **band,** but that's not important to our story.

Aunt May is the kindest person Peter knows. Peter probably wishes he could tell Aunt May about the whole **Spider-Man** thing, but he is worried that it might be too big a **SHOCK** for her.

TA-DA!

EEEK!

Now that's **love.**

Peter isn't (((**LOUD**))) and **CONFIDENT** like some other Super Heroes.

He doesn't manage **huge corporations** or know any wealthy investors.

He doesn't have specialist training as a **spy** or **assassin.**

He isn't a world-famous **SCIENTIST...**

...or genetically enhanced **super-soldier.**

New York's biggest bookworm. Or should that be bookspider...?

He's just... a kid who reads **BOOKS** and **COMICS,** works hard at *school,* and did I mention he loves **science?**

In fact, Peter's 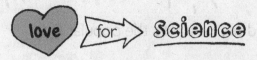 love for science

is what started off the whole Spider-Man story in the first place.

If it wasn't for science, he would never have been anything other than nerdy little Peter Parker.

And nerdy little Peter Parker is one of the kinder nicknames Peter gets called at good old

Yes, our unlikely little Super Hero is in

And **no,** he is **not** the popular kid.

Bully

Bully

Bully

Bully

Peter faces many **bullies** during his time at Midtown High. They like to pick on him for being 𝓼𝓶𝓪𝓻𝓽, or for thinking science is cool. Or just because he's

BAD AT SPORTS.

Whatever their reasons, I think we can all agree that bullies are the worst.

Peter tries to ignore them, but it can be hard when they're

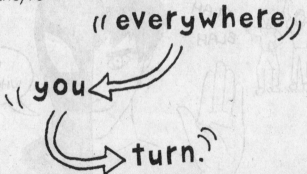

((**everywhere**))

((**you**

turn.

Before he became **Spider-Man,** school was kind of hard for Peter.

However, once he knew that he had

 **super-powers** and was actually

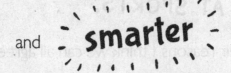

and **smarter**

than all those bullies, it became a lot easier to ignore them.

Of course, Peter did have **some** friends in high school.

Brian McKeever
Used to be a bully (boo!) but became friends with Peter (yay!).

Jessica Jones
Sssh! Has a secret crush on Peter. Sssh! Has secret powers, too.

Andy Maguire
Average guy who gained energy powers. Was Spidey's sidekick for a short while.

C. J. Vogel
Tells great jokes. Maybe C. J. stands for "Cool Joker"?

EXPERIMENTS IN RADIOACTIVITY

Ridiculously excited

Did I mention that Peter loves science? Well, just in case you forgot: this guy LOVES science. He loves it so much that he once went to an event called "Experiments in Radioactivity", just for fun. He saw some really incredible stuff!

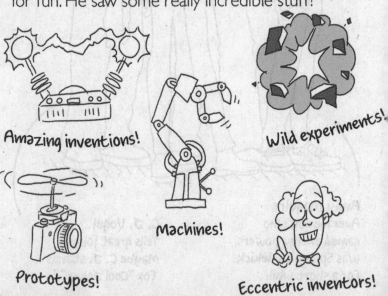

Amazing inventions!

Wild experiments!

Machines!

Prototypes!

Eccentric inventors!

And of course,

weird radioactive spiders!

Hang on, I'll back up a bit. So there was this spider, crawling along, minding its own business.

DON'T MIND ME. I'M JUST A NORMAL SPIDER.

Meanwhile, one of the machines clearly wasn't as accurate as it should have been, and –

ZAP!

– there's a radioactive spider on the loose.
I think we all know what happens next...

I hope you've never been bitten by a **spider!** It isn't fun. Luckily, this spider wasn't *poisonous* (although radioactive isn't any better).

Peter quickly started to feel **weird.**

Really weird.

So weird he had to run out of the lab to get some fresh air.

Is it just me, or is it hot in here?!

You can imagine Peter was a little **SURPRISED**
to find himself on top of a

building,

when all he had done was **jump**
out of the way of a **car.**

Super-

Super

(and

powers – tricky!

tricky!

sometimes sticky)

It didn't take long for our **spider-bite** victim to realize that his weird feelings weren't just feelings. He had somehow got...
SPIDER-POWERS!

This might take some getting used to...

That's right — he can stick to, well, everything. Like a spider, Peter can **climb walls** and hang **UPSIDE DOWN.**

He can also **JUMP** high and **leap** from place to place. But he always **lands** on his feet.

Peter gets such a thrill trying out his **new powers.** (Wouldn't you?)

He climbs tall buildings and hops from skyscraper to skyscraper. Living in **New York City** is really starting to pay off!

WARNING: DO NOT TRY THIS AT HOME! YOU DON'T HAVE SPIDER-POWERS!

On top of that, Peter has other cool, spiderlike abilities, including **super-speed,**

fast reflexes,

and **INCREDIBLE BALANCE.**

Not that unusual in **spiders,** but VERY unusual in **humans!**

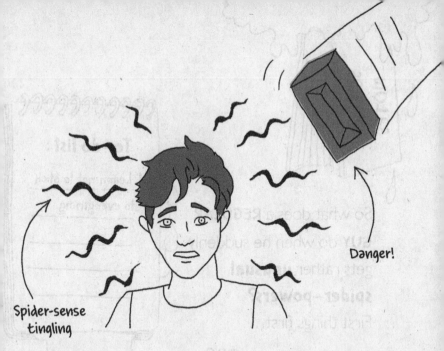

Spider-sense
tingling

Danger!

Peter also realizes he has what he calls a

"**spider-sense.**"

He gets a **feeling** about things before they happen!

It doesn't take
Peter long to
accept that he has
**super-
powers.**

But is he a
Super Hero yet?
**We'll have to wait
and see...**

SCIENCE NOTES

To-do list :

1. Learn not to stick
to everything

So what does a **REGULAR GUY** do when he suddenly gets rather **unusual spider-powers?**
First things first…

Not sticking to stuff when you are suddenly very **sticky** is pretty tough. But Peter's a smart kid, and he eventually gets the hang of it. The trick is to control the power using his mind.

Simple, really.

Once Peter has **mastered** this, he's ready to try out the rest of his new powers.

What will he do with them?

Oh, the possibilities! Super-powers give a guy so many options.

Peter could just spend all day leaping from building to building. **Talk about fun!**

He could seek **fame and fortune** – and become a **millionaire!**

Hmm... what about being a **party entertainer?** Kids would LOVE him.

Maybe he should **help** people in trouble – that's what a lot of Super Heroes seem to do.

Decisions, decisions...

That's right! He went for **fame and fortune.**

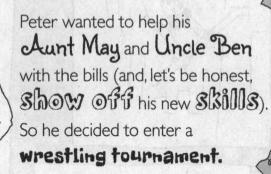

Peter wanted to help his **Aunt May** and **Uncle Ben** with the bills (and, let's be honest, **show off** his new **skills**). So he decided to enter a **wrestling tournament.**

Wearing an… **interesting** homemade costume, he was ready to wrestle.

Grrrrr!

And of course, he **won!** (The other guy had NO chance.) Everybody wanted to hear about this **new wrestling champion.**

Peter gave interviews on **TV shows,** and people were lining up to pay him **money** for his story. Could life get any better?

But **one day**, Peter had to make an important choice when he saw a **thief** in action...

STOP THE BADDIE OR DON'T STOP THE BADDIE?

And here's where Peter **really** let himself down. He decided that stopping the villain *wasn't his problem.*

He went home, thinking no more about it. But…

Peter was **shocked** to discover that the same **villain** he'd let escape had killed his beloved **Uncle Ben.**

This was an eye-opening moment for Peter.
He realized that using his powers to help people was ALWAYS his business.

Peter was **devastated** about **Uncle Ben**.
But he made a decision, then and there.
He was going to use his powers for good.

And he remembered
something **Uncle Ben**
always used to say…

WITH
GREAT
POWER
THERE MUST
ALSO COME
GREAT
RESPONSIBILITY.

Now it was time **to get serious** about becoming a Super Hero. **And that means...**

1. Costume
2. Gadgets
3. ~~Aunt May's birthday~~ Oops, wrong list!
4. Get out there and HELP people

There are lots of **villains** in New York City, and Peter hopes he can **help** make the city a **better place**.

WANTED

WANTED
Vulture

WANTED
Doctor Octopus

WANTED
Green Goblin

WANTED
Rhino

WANTED
Lizard

But let's not get ahead of ourselves! Like all **nerdy, organized** Super Heroes, Peter works his way through his to-do list, starting with number one…

Peter decided to go with a spider theme for his first, homemade Spider-Man costume.
Makes perfect sense.

Swimming goggles

Basic mask

Loose-fitting hoodie

Standard issue trainers

But it was – how can I put it nicely? – not that great.
YOU NEED A BETTER COSTUME, PETER!

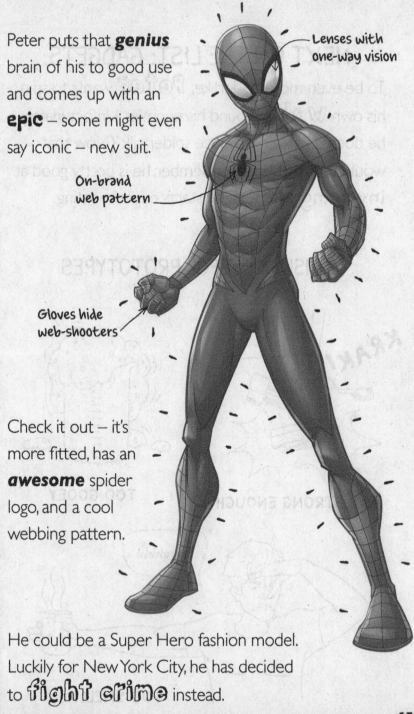

Peter puts that **genius** brain of his to good use and comes up with an **epic** – some might even say iconic – new suit.

Lenses with one-way vision

On-brand web pattern

Gloves hide web-shooters

Check it out – it's more fitted, has an **awesome** spider logo, and a cool webbing pattern.

He could be a Super Hero fashion model. Luckily for New York City, he has decided to **fight crime** instead.

NEXT ON THE LIST: GADGETS.

To be even more spiderlike, **Peter** wants to spin his own **webs** around his enemies. Unfortunately, he doesn't actually produce spider silk. (Now that would be **COOL!**) But remember, he is pretty good at **inventing stuff,** so he starts experimenting.

UNSUCCESSFUL PROTOTYPES

NOT STRONG ENOUGH

TOO GOOEY

Errrghhh!

TOO SMELLY

First, Peter invents his own web-fluid: a **super sticky, DURABLE, elastic** material that dissolves after about an hour. Useful for Super Heroes and not much else. **PERFECT!**

Next, he **makes** a pair of **web-shooters** that snap around his wrists. If he presses the trigger on his palms twice, the web-fluid **SHOOTS** out. Simple and brilliant!

I know who my first target will be!

FINALLY, Spider-Man is ready to **STOP** the **bad guys.** And it feels **good!**

Maybe not as good as just chilling and watching TV, but hey. (Okay, okay, **JUST KIDDING.**)

SATURDAY AFTERNOON, 2:30PM...

Spidey can hold his head up **HIGH** as he
tries to change the **world for the better.**
And we get to see his Spidey suit
and awesome gadgets in ACTION.
All we need now are some **bad guys...**

Those Sly

GRRRRR!

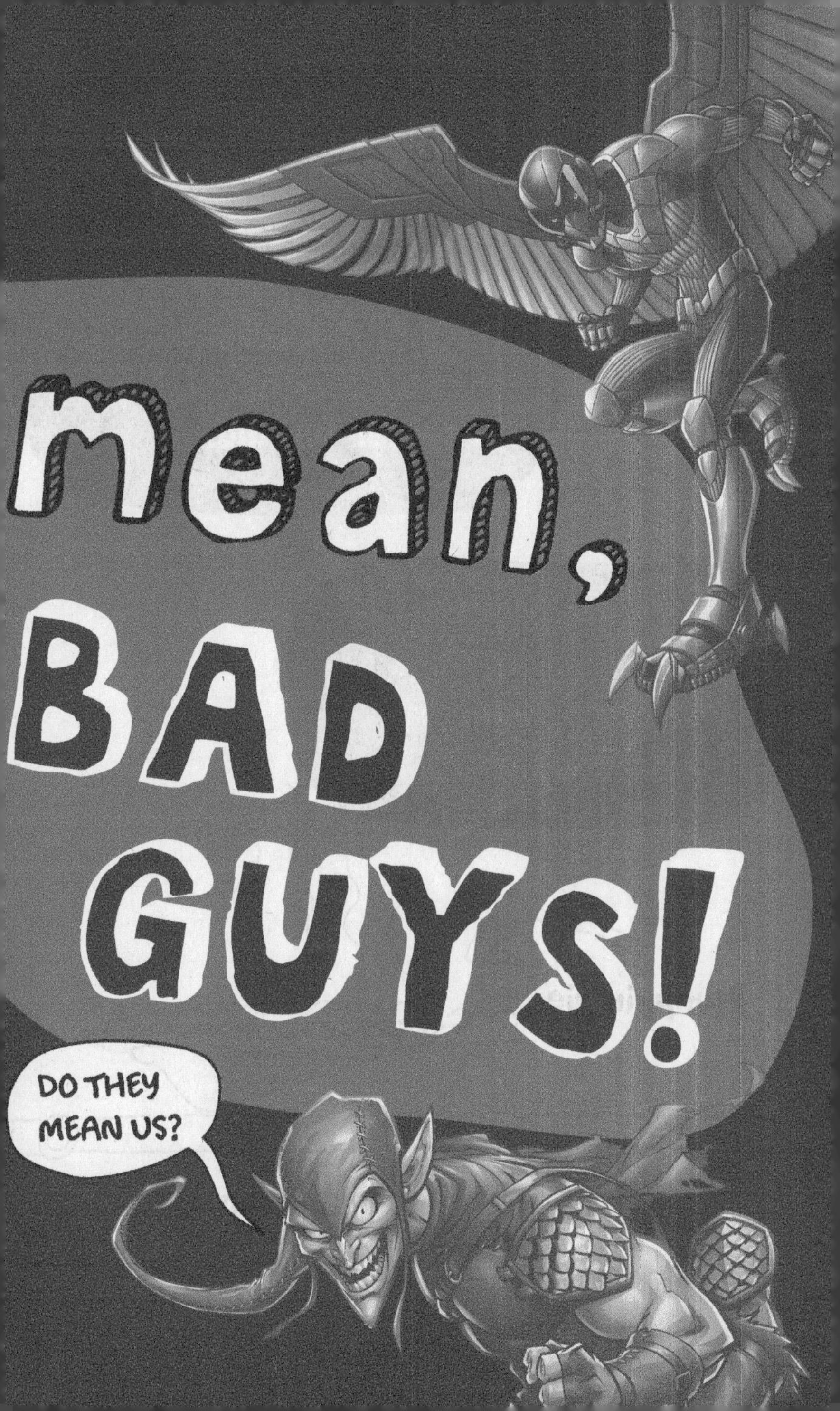
mean,
BAD
GUYS!
DO THEY MEAN US?

It turns out there are actually quite a lot of **bad guys** in **New York City.** But let's call them what they really are: **Super Villains.** That's right. Even more evil than a **regular baddie.**

Spidey has faced lots of Super Villains in his time. And he always has one **main** goal: **to stop them.**

Pumpkin pie

Trapdoor

You may have heard of the

Green Goblin.

He causes havoc across **New York City** and doesn't care who he hurts. Some might say he is Spider-Man's arch-enemy.

The Green Goblin isn't his real name, of course. His real name is much less exciting: **Norman Osborn.**

NORMAN was just a **genius businessman,** until he took a **serum** to give himself **super-strength** But the serum wasn't quite perfect, and it gave him **super-powers,** including **amazing agility, stamina,** and **durability.**

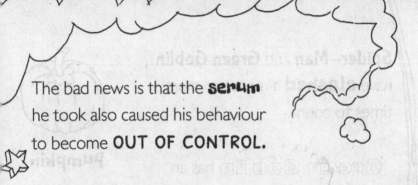

The bad news is that the **serum** he took also caused his behaviour to become **OUT OF CONTROL.**

Spider-Man and **Green Goblin** have **clashed** almost too many times to count.

Green Goblin has an incredible number of **GADGETS** and **WEAPONS.** His favourite are the **pumpkin bombs.** They might sound silly, but believe me, they are **really** effective.

Pumpkin

Pumpkin Bomb

Spider-Man doesn't have as many gadgets, but he DOES have **web-shooters** – which are awesome, as we know – so it's a pretty even match.

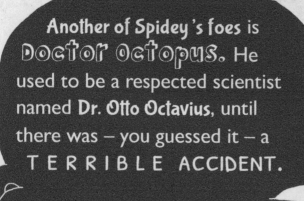

Another of Spidey's foes is **DOCTOR OCTOPUS.** He used to be a respected scientist named **Dr. Otto Octavius,** until there was – you guessed it – a TERRIBLE ACCIDENT.

Four **mechanical arms** became attached to his body. OUCH!

#1

As if that wasn't **bad** enough, the accident made him even more **arrogant** than he already was. Now his biggest goal is to prove himself the **greatest villain in the world.**

Luckily for the **world,** one of Spider-Man's biggest goals is to **STOP** this guy.

Canned SQUID

Rhino

used to be a **thug** named **Aleksei Sytsevich**. He was so **loyal** to the **Mafia** that he let them carry out experiments on him. One of these experiments attached a **SUPER-STRONG ARMOUR,** modelled on the **SKIN OF A RHINO,** to his body.

Good Rhino

Bad Rhino

Sorry, but did you see Spider-Man come this way?

Now his body may have **superhuman strength,** but Rhino is still not **super smart.** So when he comes up against Spider-Man in battle, Spider-Man realizes he can win simply by **outthinking** the beast.

Hmmm... shall I move left or right?

As long as he doesn't find himself on the sharp end of **Rhino's horn,** Spidey knows he can **DEFEAT** him in any battle, any place, any time.

Meet **Vulture!**

Well, actually, don't. **Adrian Toomes** is a **genius engineer,** but he's also a **sneaky thief** known as **Vulture.**

His winged suit has built-in **razor-sharp talons,** and it gives him superhuman strength. Worst of all (for the citizens of New York), it also allows him to **fly.**

Lizard, on the other hand, didn't mean to turn himself into a **Super Villain.** Scientist and surgeon **Curt Connors** just wanted to **regrow** his arm that he lost while serving as a battlefield medic.

Er, that's not supposed to happen...

Unfortunately, the **serum** he used – which was made of **lizard DNA** – kept on working after his arm **regrew,** turning him into a **wild reptilian creature.**

Have you heard of **Wilson Fisk?** Of course you have – he's the **MAYOR OF NEW YORK CITY.** Oh yes, he's also the leader of a **criminal** empire that terrorizes the city.

SPIDEY'S TO-DO LIST

1. DEFEAT KINGPIN
2. HAND HIM OVER TO THE POLICE
3. FIND ESCAPED KINGPIN
4. HAND HIM OVER TO POLICE (AGAIN)
5. REPEAT

Known as **Kingpin,** Fisk is one of Spider-Man's greatest **FOES.** The two clash again and again as Spidey tries to spoil Kingpin's latest **greedy, illegal plot.**

Kingpin is **BIG,** strong, and a **master of combat.** He's not afraid of fighting anyone – even **Super Heroes.**

Worst of all, Kingpin has so much **INFLUENCE** and *money* (for lawyers and bribes) that he usually avoids ending up in jail.

Crime is on the rise – and therefore so are our profits.

You will do these things, or your life will be very unpleasant.

If some maniac has decided to rid me of Spider-Man, why should I interfere?

Spider-Man might have built a reputation as an **AMAZING** Super Hero, but that doesn't mean he has everything figured out.

TAKE THAT ONE TIME he was **KIDNAPPED** with some other Super Heroes and ended up on a distant planet.

That sounds bad, right? But it gets worse...

Spider-Man found a really **COOL** **BLACK SPIDEY-THEMED COSTUME.**

Oh wow! This is a stroke of luck!

okay, so what's the **problem?** Well, Spidey discovered that the **costume** wasn't a costume at all. It was actually an

EVIL ALIEN PARASITE!

The new, **black costume** seemed to enhance Spidey's skills at first.

But eventually, Peter realized that it was actually trying to take over his **body** and his **mind.** Not so good.

I HATE SPIDER-MAN

+

alien parasite

Peter managed to get rid of the alien, but the alien **wasn't gone.** It went and bonded permanently with **EDDIE BROCK.**

Eddie already held a **grudge** against
Spider-Man after Peter embarrassed Eddie years
earlier. So he was more than happy to suddenly
gain Spidey powers of his own! He took on the
very villainous name, Venom.

Venom isn't the only spider-themed **villain.** There are plenty more out there who are not big fans of **Spider-Man** and his quest for justice.

Carnage is an alien life-form created by Venom. Like Venom, Carnage can bond with a human, giving them super-powers.

Unfortunately for the world, **_Carnage_** bonded with a dangerous criminal named **CLETUS KASADY**.

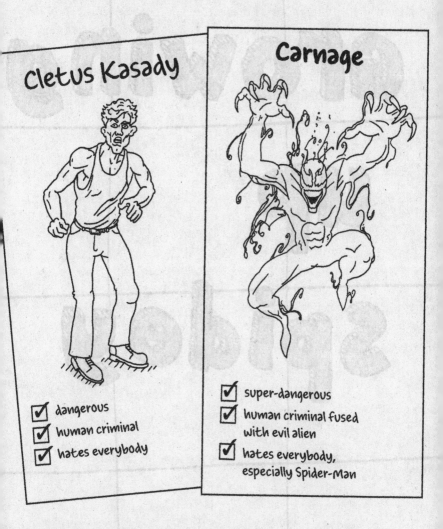

Cletus Kasady

- ✓ dangerous
- ✓ human criminal
- ✓ hates everybody

Carnage

- ✓ super-dangerous
- ✓ human criminal fused with evil alien
- ✓ hates everybody, especially Spider-Man

Now with spider-powers, Carnage is even more **unpredictable** and **dangerous** than Cletus was. And that's saying something!

Growing up Spidey

So what's it **really** like being a **SUPER HERO?** It's not all **web-slinging** and **wall-climbing,** I can tell you that! There's something called **real life,** remember?

Yes, the boiler's broken...

Peter Parker grows up, and he needs to get a **job** (being a Spider-Man isn't exactly a paid position). He needs to look after **AUNT MAY**, pay the **bills,** and **pretend** to the world he's not a masked Super Hero.

You know, all the usual real-life stuff.

PETER has a secret **talent** for taking **pictures,** so he applies to be a **photographer** for his local paper,

The Daily Bugle.

How do you always know where Spider-Man will be to get such great shots?

Just lucky, I guess.

Peter **TAKES GREAT PHOTOS** to accompany **news stories.** But he proves **surprisingly good** at capturing **exclusive** photos of **Spider-Man.** I wonder why…

Here's a top tip for you: try not to work for someone who thinks your **alter ego is a MENACE.** Oops. I'm talking about newspaper editor-in-chief,

J. Jonah Jameson.

He likes to play by the rules. He thinks **Spidey** just gets in the way and should **LEAVE VILLAIN-CATCHING** to the

POLICE

It can be tricky for Peter to listen while his boss rants about everything that is **wrong** with **Spider-Man.**

Still, a good Super Hero never reveals his real identity.

Oh no, not this again...

After high school, **PETER** goes off to **Empire State University** to study...

you guessed it...

science.

 Biophysics, to be exact.

He meets **people who like science** as much as he does and makes **friends** with some of them.

HARRY OSBORN is Peter's best friend, even though things get a bit **complicated** when Peter realizes who **Harry's dad** is.

It's Norman Osborn – the Green Goblin!

Peter and Harry are from completely different worlds. **Harry's dad** is **super-rich** but does not have a lot of patience for his son. **Aunt May** might not have much, but she **loves** Peter with all her **heart.**

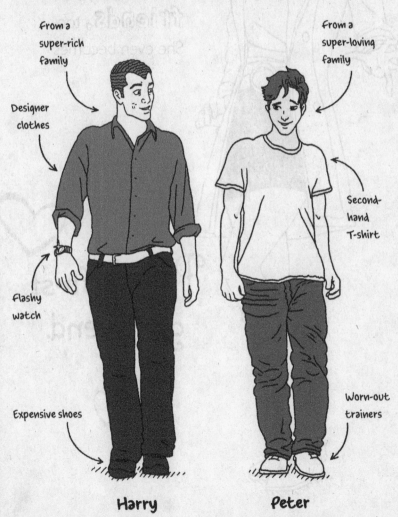

From a super-rich family

Designer clothes

Flashy watch

Expensive shoes

From a super-loving family

Second-hand T-shirt

Worn-out trainers

Harry

Peter

One of **Harry's** other friends is a girl named **Gwen Stacy.** Peter and Gwen became **close friends,** too. She even becomes

Peter's first girlfriend.

Unfortunately, being Spider-Man's girlfriend can put you in **danger** –

He he he!

Eeek!

Told you!

even if you don't know that he is **Spider-Man.**

You see, **Super Villains** don't care **WHO KNOWS WHAT.** All they know is that if Spider-Man cares about someone, **that someone** makes a very **good target.**

Having **FRIENDS** is a good thing, but it does make being a Super Hero a little **bit trickier.**

For one thing, Peter has to make sure he doesn't leave his **web-shooters** lying around. He also has to work hard to keep his **secret identity** a <u>**secret**</u>.

So, he has a **few tips** up **his spidey-sleeves:**

1. **Always** have an **alibi**
2. **REMEMBER** to change out of your **Spidey suit** before **meeting up** with your **friends**
3. When someone yells out, "HEY, SPIDER-MAN!" **don't answer**

And perhaps the most important tip of all...

Sometimes, keeping secrets from your friends isn't just **difficult** – it can be downright **DANGEROUS**. Especially when the **secrets** start to come **OUT!**

When **Harry** discovers that his dad is the **Green Goblin,** he kind of overlooks the fact that the Green Goblin is **"NOT SO NICE."** Then his father dies, and Harry turns his anger towards Spider-Man, blaming him for what happened.

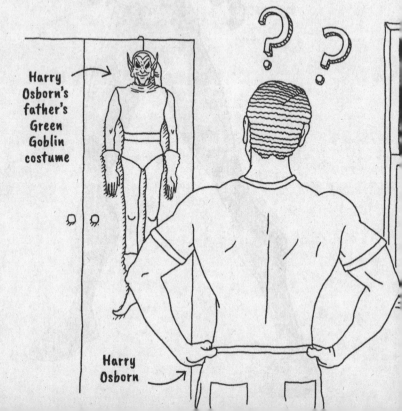

Harry Osborn's father's Green Goblin costume

Harry Osborn

AND THEN… Harry finds out that Spidey is none other than his best friend and roommate, **Peter Parker!** An angry Harry takes on the Green Goblin **persona,** but Peter doesn't want to **fight** his BEST FRIEND.

95

Spider-Man lives an exciting life,

but don't forget he has a real life, too.
Peter finds love with **Mary Jane Watson,**
or **MJ,** as everyone calls her.

And for once, **Spidey** doesn't have to hide who he
really is because **MJ knows the truth:** that under
the red mask, it's **Peter Parker.**

She's known this for many years.
She spotted **Spider-Man**
creeping out of Peter's bedroom
window the night **Uncle
Ben** was killed.

Gasp!

Talk about being good
at keeping **secrets!**
These two are **perfect**
for each other.

Peter has a few different jobs over the years.

He teaches at **EMPIRE STATE UNIVERSITY,** and he also has a stint as a **teaching assistant** at **Midtown High.**

Later, Peter gets the job of his **dreams** at a state-of-the-art research facility called **Horizon Labs.**

Peter makes the most of his time here to invent **awesome new gadgets** and suits for Spider-Man. Somehow, the genius scientists at Horizon don't catch on that Peter is Spidey.

Oh wow, so cool. Looks like something Spider-Man would use.

What? Wh-who? Never heard of him...

I'm not sure what they **DO THINK,** but I probably wouldn't hire any of them as a **detective!**

GUESS who's been watching **Spider-Man** on the news?

I think we can call **THIS GUY** a *fan.*

Yes, that's right. It's **Tony Stark.**

When the one and only **Iron Man** invites Spidey to team up with the **Avengers Super Hero team,** how can Spidey say **NO?**

Spidey even gets his own

Iron Spider Armor,

which enhances all of his **super-powers, and** lets him **fly!**

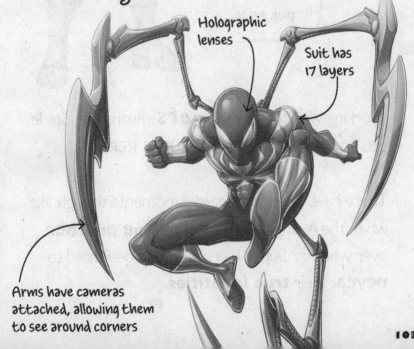

Holographic lenses

Suit has 17 layers

Arms have cameras attached, allowing them to see around corners

Team Captain America

I need to pick a side...

Working with the **Avengers** means that Spidey gets to hang out with other **SUPER HEROES.**

There have been some sticky moments, though, like when the Avengers **turned on one another** over whether Super Heroes should be forced to **reveal** their *true identities.*

Spidey had to **pick a side,** and it has affected his friendship with **TONY STARK.**

Doc Ock

Still, Spidey did help the Avengers out when *Doctor Octopus* took over their bodies and tried to ***destroy the world,*** so maybe they're **EVEN.**

Spidey has also **teamed up** with some spider-themed **Super Heroes** over the years.

CINDY MOON was actually bitten by the same spider as Peter. Her spider-powers are slightly different from Peter's, though: she can produce her own spider webs…

… from her fingertips!

I wish I could do that!

But **Cindy** was targeted by the **Super Villain Morlun,** so she hid herself away for years. When Peter heard about her, he **RESCUED HER** and she took the **SUPER HERO NAME...**

Silk

Unfortunately, **MORLUN** was still a threat, despite Peter defeating him. *But we'll get to that later!*

HER PARENTS were **scientists** who carried out lots of **spider-y and radiation-y** (those are the **technical terms,** ahem) experiments, to try to heal Jessica when she was **ILL.** This resulted in accidentally giving her super-powers!

Jessica grew up to be a **private detective** and Super Hero known as:

Spider-Woman.

She was also **tricked into joining** a group of **Super Villains,** but let's not get into that. **All that matters** is that she is a **Super Hero** now.

After so many years as **SPIDER-MAN**, Peter has learned a lot about *responsibility,* being **brave,** living a double life, and stopping Super Villains.

He knows that life's one big juggling act. He knows that sometimes, despite everything you do, **the bad guy wins.** He knows that Kingpin will, somehow, always manage to **ESCAPE.**

He also knows to be on the lookout for danger and to **EXPECT THE UNEXPECTED.** But sometimes something comes along that even Spider-Man isn't prepared for…

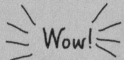
Wow!

Talk about surprises! Spider-Man can't believe it when he meets a **whole load of other** Spideys from a whole load of different

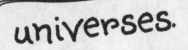
universes.

Ever get the feeling someone's copying your style?

Ghost-Spider

Miles Morales

There's another **Spider-Man,** but he isn't Peter Parker at all — he is a teenager named **MILES MORALES.** Even stranger is the Super Hero known as **Ghost-Spider.** Her real name is **GWEN STACY.** **Yes, you read that right.** In Ghost-Spider's universe, **she** was the one bitten by a **radioactive spider.**

Spider-Man 2099

I do get around a bit!

She does have a friend named Peter Parker, but she is the

Super Hero,

not him.

Spider-Girl

And that's not all. There's also **Spider-Girl** (another teenager with spidey-powers),

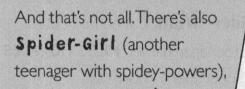

Spider-Man 2099 (from the future),

SP//dr (a robot spider controlled by a girl named Peni Parker),

Spider-Ham (yes, he's a pig – what's your point?),

Spider-UK
(Spider-Man from the UK, correct),

and Spider-Man: India
(can you guess where he's from?).

When Peter gets over the **shock** of meeting other spider Super Heroes, he is honoured to **join forces** with them.

This **strange** but POWERFUL collection of spider Super Heroes team up to stop a seriously **BAD GUY.** This Super Villain is known as **Morlun.**

Morlun is a **creepy,** DANGEROUS

ENERGY VAMPIRE.

He feeds on super-powered people, and he wants to **feast** on SPIDER-MAN!

Gross!!

So that's where all my energy's gone!

Spider-Man defeated **Morlun** once before, but now the villain is back and he is attacking **all** spider heroes, from **all** universes. **Yikes!**

Peter and his army of spider friends **DEFEAT** Morlun, although they can't be sure that he is gone forever.

SPIDERS ASSEMBLE!

Hmm, that's a catchy phrase...

Being a **Super Hero** isn't **SUPER** all the time. There are **disadvantages** to having **super-secret spider super-powers.**

For example, not being able to take credit for all the **GOOD** you do, having to **lie** to your friends, having to lie to **Aunt May,** having to sometimes run really, **REALLY** fast, and even missing your friends' **birthday parties** without being able to give a reason **WHY.**

You're late for dinner again, Peter.

Sorry, Aunt May. Rhino –

A rhino?!

Er, yes. One escaped from the, erm... zoo.

RHINO ARRESTED

I'm going to be late!

Still, Peter wouldn't change his **secret identity** for **ANYTHING.** He feels **PROUD** every time he defeats a *villain* and makes the world that **little bit <u>safer.</u>**

Glossary

Agility
The ability to move quickly and precisely.

Alibi
An excuse that proves innocence.

Allies
Friends, or people who fight alongside others.

Archenemy
Someone or something's biggest foe.

Arrogant
When people behave as if they are more important than others.

Assassin
Someone who kills others, often in exchange for money.

Athletic
Healthy and good at sports.

Corporation
A large company.

Devastated
Very, very upset and sad.

Durability
Strength to endure.

Enhance
Make better.

I ♥ SCIENCE

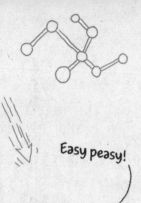

Easy peasy!

Foolproof
A plan or action that is so easy that it cannot go wrong.

Iconic
Well known and often popular.

Illegal
Not allowed by law.

Influence
The power to affect people or things, such as behaviour or choices.

Investor
Somebody who puts time or money into something, such as a business, to make profit.

Mafia
A criminal organization who help and protect each other.

Mastered
When someone is very good at an activity, usually through practise.

Mechanical
Operates like a machine.

Parasite
A living being that feeds on another living being to survive.

Poisonous
A harmful substance that can cause illness or death.

THWIP!

Prototypes
An example of a machine or product.

Radioactive
A kind of energy that can be very dangerous in large amounts.

Reflexes
Actions your body makes without thinking.

Reptilian
Like a reptile in looks or behaviour. Snakes are a type of reptile.

Reputation
How someone or something is thought of by others, often based on past behaviour.

Respected
Someone or something that others have a high opinion of.

Responsibility
A job that you have to do.

Stamina
The physical ability to do something for a long time.

FRIENDLY
NEIGHBOURHOOD
SPIDER-MAN

$e=mc^2$

Technical term
The formal name for a thing, process, or activity.

Terrorize
Cause fear among people, often through violence.

(BAD GUY ALERT!)

Unpredictable
Behave in a way that changes quickly and often.

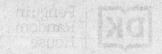

Senior Editor Emma Grange
Editor Vicky Armstrong
Project Art Editors Jon Hall and Stefan Georgiou
Senior Production Editor Jennifer Murray
Senior Production Controller Mary Slater
Managing Editor Sarah Harland
Managing Art Editor Vicky Short
Publishing Director Mark Searle

Illustrations by Dan Crisp and Jon Hall

DK would like to thank Caitlin O'Connell and Jeff Youngquist at Marvel;
Chelsea Alon at Disney; Jennette ElNaggar for editorial help; Ray Bryant,
Guy Harvey, Gary Hyde, Nathan Martin, and David McDonald for design
assistance; Julie Ferris and Lisa Lanzarini; and Shari Last for her writing.

First published in Great Britain in 2021 by
Dorling Kindersley Limited
One Embassy Gardens, 8 Viaduct Gardens,
London SW11 7BW

The authorised representative in the EEA is
Dorling Kindersley Verlag GmbH. Arnulfstr. 124,
80636 Munich, Germany

10 9 8 7 6 5 4 3 2 1
003–321958–June/2021

A CIP catalogue record for this book is available
from the British Library.
ISBN 978-0-24146-971-2

Printed in the UK

For the curious

www.dk.com
www.marvel.com

MIX
Paper from
responsible sources
FSC™ C018179
www.fsc.org

This book is made from
Forest Stewardship Council™
certified paper – one small
step in DK's commitment
to a sustainable future.